Advi__

to those who participate in Dawah
along with the

Tableeghi Jamaat

by Sajid A. Kayum

Published by
Quran Sunnah Educational Programs
www.qsep.com

Sunnah Bookstore
On the Frontline For Authenticity

Advice to those who participate in Dawah along with the Tableeghi Jamaat

1ˢᵗ Edition © QSEP

ISBN: 978-0-9571668-1-3

Printed and distributed by:
Sunnah Bookstore
42a Maynard Road
Leicester
England, LE2 0AN
www.sunnahbookstore.com
admin@sunnahbookstore.com

With the kind permission of:
Quran Sunnah Educational Programs
www.qsep.com
qsep@gmail.com

Contents

Knowledge
is necessary to fulfill
the responsibility of

Dawah

Dawah to Allah (سبحانه و تعالى) is indeed a lofty deed which leads to great benefit for the Muslim Ummah. Its purpose is to rectify the religious and worldly affairs of the people, so that their lives are in accordance with the guidance that has been revealed by Allah (سبحانه و تعالى).

Dawah is an endeavor and a means to great reward and honor, as the Messenger of Allah ﷺ said to Alee ibn Abi Talib (رضى الله عنه) on the day of Khaybar, "By Allah! If a single person embraces Islam at your hands - that will be better for you than red camels."

[Saheeh al-Bukharee (52/192)]

However, to be entitled to this reward, it is essential that the one who calls people to righteousness **should have the correct understanding of what he is calling to** - though he does not have to know the entire religion - as Allah's Messenger ﷺ said,

"Convey from me, even if it is one ayah."

[Saheeh al-Bukharee (3461)]

Al-Hafidh ibn Hajar (رحمه الله) said explaining the words, "even if it is one ayah" - so that everyone who heard him ﷺ would hasten to convey whatever he heard of the ayaat - even if it was very little - so that in this manner, everything that he ﷺ brought would be conveyed.

[See, Fathul-Baree]

Shaikh Ibn Uthaimeen (رحمه الله) explained,

"If a person understands what he is calling people to, it makes no difference whether he is a great and prominent scholar or a seeker of knowledge, who is serious in his pursuit thereof, or a regular person who has certain knowledge of the issue in question.

The Messenger ﷺ said, "Convey from me, even if it is one ayah," and he ﷺ did not stipulate that the caller to Allah should reach a high level of knowledge, but it is essential that he should have knowledge of that which he is calling the people to. But Dawah based on ignorance or emotion is not permissible."

[Fatawa Ulama al-Balad al-Haraam (p. 329)]

"It is also declared Haraam (forbidden) to say or discuss things about which one does not have knowledge, as Allah (سبحانه و تعالى) says,

2

"Say (O Muhammad ﷺ), '(But) the things that my Lord has indeed forbidden are al-Fawahish (great evil sins) whether committed openly or secretly, sins (of all kinds), unrighteous oppression, joining partners (in worship) with Allah for which He has given no authority, and saying things about Allah of which you have no knowledge.'"

[Soorah al-A'raaf (7): 33]

...and His (سبحانه و تعالى) Saying,

"Follow not that of which you have no knowledge."

[Soorah al-Isra (17): 36]

There are also other texts (from the Qur'aan and the Sunnah) bearing the same meaning, **which encourage the conveyance of the Message of Islam and caution against speaking without knowledge."**

[Permanent Committee Fatawa (qsep 305)]

Amongst the ayaat that lay the foundation for the correct manner of Dawah is Allah's Order to His Messenger ﷺ to proclaim,

"Say (O Muhammad ﷺ), 'This is my way. I invite unto Allah with sure knowledge, I and whosoever follows me (also must invite others to Allah).'"

[Soorah Yoosuf (12): 108]

Imaam Ibn Katheer (رحمه الله) writes,

"(In this ayah), Allah orders His Messenger ﷺ to say to mankind and the Jinn that this is his way - meaning his method, path and Sunnah; focused upon calling to the testimony, 'there is no deity worthy of worship except Allah alone, (the One) without partners.'

The Messenger ﷺ calls to this testimony with sure knowledge, certainty and firm evidence. He ﷺ calls to this way, and those who

3

follow him call to what Allah's Messenger ﷺ (called to - with sure knowledge, certainty and evidence, whether logical or religious evidence."   [Tafseer Ibn Katheer]

"Knowledge is what Allah says in His Book, or what His Messenger ﷺ says in his Saheeh (authentic) Sunnah.

So one should learn the Qur'aan and the Sunnah to find out what Allah has enjoined and what Allah has forbidden, and to know the way in which the Messenger ﷺ called people to Allah and denounced evil, and the way in which his Companions gave Dawah.

One can gain insight into this by studying the books of Hadeeth, and paying attention to the Qur'aan, and studying the words of the scholars on the subject because they have discussed it in-depth and explained what is obligatory.

The one who wants to set himself up as a caller must pay attention to this matter to have proper insight into the Book of Allah and the Sunnah of His Messenger ﷺ - so that he places things in their right places .

He will (thus,) call people to good when it is appropriate, and enjoin what is good when it is appropriate, with insight and knowledge, (And) that he will not denounce evil in a way that is more evil than it, and that he will not enjoin what is good in a manner that will result in an evil worse than not doing the good thing.

The point is that it is essential for the caller to Allah to have knowledge so that he does things properly."

[Majmoo Fatawa Ibn Baaz (27/340)]

Therefore, while Dawah is essential, and one need not be a scholar to engage in it - if you have taken it upon yourself to invite others to good, you must have knowledge about it, else from the most evil of matters is:

- Speaking about Allah without knowledge
- Enjoining the good in a manner that will result in a greater evil.

Advice to those who participate
in Dawah along with the
Tableeghi Jamaat

So, you have the noble intention to rectify the affairs of the people, and have chosen to do this by means of participation in the activities of the Tableeghi Jamaat – **then, here are a few important matters that you should be aware of about Tableeghi Jamaat's activities**, so that your choice is based on the right information and the correct perspective;

- Perhaps, someone exaggerated the status of a group's activities; calling it the work of the Sahabah - **and it may not be so.**
- Perhaps, someone exaggerated the reward of doing certain actions - **and they may not have any proofs for their claim.**
- Perhaps, you are unaware of the gross mistakes in the teachings of a group - **and you unknowingly participate in it.**

- Perhaps, you hope that the activities of a group can bring about religious Islaah (reformation) in the lives of the Muslims - **and you have been deceived into believing this.**

Methodology
of the Discussion

Hereunder is a brief history of our discussions with brothers associated with the Tableeghi Jamaat. It will explain the methodology adopted for the discussions to follow, and serve as a response to some commonly raised arguments.

This compilation started after we encountered a few tableeghi brothers persistent on recruiting a few friends of ours in the Tableeghi Jamaat, while they were already involved in studying the Deen and in Dawah - though in a manner different from the Tableeghi way.

The Tableeghi brothers insisted that the only correct way of Dawah was their way - as had been handed down by their elders.

We explained to these brothers that our way was to study the books of Aqeedah, general Fiqh, Tafseer ibn Katheer, etc., - mostly under the supervision of students of knowledge. And we did do our part in Dawah amongst family, friends and colleagues - basically by way of exchanging books and tapes, and by general discussions and clarifications.

When pressed as to why we were averse to joining them, we cited **some apparent and observed flaws in the way of the Tableeghi Jamaat,** among them:

- **They rely too much on story-telling in the Tableeghi Jamaat,** whether it is stories of their buzurgs (elders) or strange occurrences that happen during Tableeghi activities (karguzari).

- **Veteran Jamaat members are seen explaining Islamic concepts by means of everyday examples (like trains, buses, etc.), instead of Tafseer and Hadeeth.**

  Carelessness in quoting from the Qur'aan and the Sunnah are widespread, such that speakers bundle up Qur'aan, Hadeeth and stories together, and the listener has no clue as to what is what.

  At times, we also find, popular sayings being presented as the Hadeeth of Allah's Messenger ﷺ.

- **Complete new-comers are encouraged to speak in matters of the Deen,** and they explain Islamic concepts in light of personal experiences, and often say that which is either false or inappropriate.

  No objection is raised to such talk, as long as it is centered on the basic idea of going out with the tableeghis for three-days, forty-days, etc.

  This can be quiet frustrating for someone, who is serious in studying the Deen, and is concerned about the authenticity of what is being said in the name of Allah (سبحانه و تعالى).

- **Though the subjects of Islamic learning are varied, the one who associates with this Jamaat hardly makes any progress in his knowledge** because the education there does not go beyond the six-points of tableegh and readings from Fazaail-e-Aamaal.

- **Members of the Tableeghi Jamaat often impose participation on the people without any consideration** for their schedule or busyness.

  They greatly exaggerate the virtues of participation with them and unjustifiably make a person feel guilty for his lack of involvement.

- **Deception was being used to entice people into the 'three-day routine';** - Veteran tableeghis, who had already registered themselves for the activity, would continually re-register themselves at every mosque to give the impression that a lot of people are participating, and so the one being called should not be left out.

- Often we **found an exaggerated involvement in Tableeghi activities** to the extent that individuals were encroaching upon the rights of their family and neglecting the upbringing of their children. Many youngsters were neglecting their education and taking a defeatist attitude towards life.

Though these problems are well-known, our discussion did not head anywhere because our Tableeghi brothers simply denied any such problem - although they themselves were prime examples of these flaws!

Our next approach was to rely more on textual evidences instead of practical apparent problems. We thus, prepared a few notes based on

Fazaail-e-Aamaal to show that it contains stories that contradict Islaı teachings and promote 'bareilwi-type' superstitions.

The idea was that since Fazaail-e-Aamaal is widely read in tableeghi circles, no one would deny the significance of this book or its references.

We also insisted that when responding to us, the Tableeghi brothers should not make up their own replies - but instead go back to the seniors of their organization, and ask for their response - because what carries weight is the position of the Jamaat, and not arguments that someone makes up on the fly.

The response of the Tableeghi brothers after consultation was that **Fazaail-e-Aamaal's stories were not directed towards teaching Aqeedah (beliefs) - but were aimed at encouraging righteous actions.** Hence, they disassociated themselves and the Tableeghi Jamaat from the Aqeedah in those stories.

You should know that the **Aqeedah (creed, beliefs) being promoted in the stories of Fazaail-e-Aamaal are well-accepted standpoints amongst the Deobandi elders,** as we shall demonstrate during the course of this book. But being unaware of this at the time, our argument was...

You claim to reach out to those, whom you yourselves describe as 'not knowing even the kalimah', and you are well-aware of them being engrossed in grave-worship and superstitions.

So, **can you honestly say that when these stories are read out to such ignorant people, that they will only take encouragement for righteous action from these stories, and effectively ignore the false Aqeedah that is endorsed in them?**

letely ignorant individuals, even long-timers in the Jamaat ding these corrupt views, and when asked for proof, they at Fazaail-e-Aamaal.

For instance, reciting the Kalimah seventy thousand times to save someone who died, from punishment in the hereafter. This act of worship is based on a story from Fazaail-e-Aamaal, and not from the Sunnah.

The discussions ended.

Years later, another country, another study circle being persuaded by a group of veteran Tableeghi brothers to join them - The same discussions started, and headed the same way. And these Tableeghi brothers too, repeated that Fazaail-e-Aamaal and the Jamaat only encourage righteous actions, and do not teach Aqeedah.

This time, however, we were able to show from the books of Deobandi elders that the Aqeedah, which Fazaail-e-Aamaal was promoting in those stories, was in fact, agreed-upon beliefs of the Deobandis.

These stories in Fazaail-e-Aamaal were not there by chance or by accident. Rather they were subtly introducing the masses to the beliefs, soofee concepts and attitudes that make up the Deobandi ideology.

The tableeghi brothers responded by saying that their Jamaat had nothing to do with Deoband, rather something called the Tableeghi Jamaat did not even exist!!! A few people going about their business doing Islaah (rectification) became popularly known as Tableeghi Jamaat.

This of course, is totally untrue. **The 'Tableeghi Jamaat' is the name of a specific group - with leaders (amirs), centers and activities that** involve traveling to pre-decided locations, with a pre-defined syllabus, for fixed days, and with one book - Fazaail-e-Aamaal.

It was founded by Moulana Ilyas in the 1920s, and has been directed since by the Deobandis. The members of the group take the oath of allegiance (bay'ah) to the amir (head) of the Jamaat. These are all signs of an organized group with a specific ideology.

The brothers backed down from their disassociation with the Deobandis, but since our objections were similar to those one would usually associate with grave worshipers (like calling upon the Messenger ﷺ at his grave, complaining to the engraved and seeking spiritual benefit from the dead, believing that majzoobs[1] are aware of matters between Allah and his slaves, etc.), **the brothers could only assume that these were past views that are no longer held by the Tableeghi Jamaat or the Deobandis.**

Many similar discussions with different groups of Tableeghi brothers were to follow, and the same pattern of thoughtless denials, making up arguments on the fly, and speaking on matters of the Deen without knowledge continued.

Most of these brothers were neither lying nor intentionally deceiving. Rather, their carelessness and imprudence was a result of the tarbeeyah (training) they had received from the **Tableeghi Jamaat - where all that**

---

[1]Sometimes the insanity caused by the Sufi's physical and mental abuse is permanent. People in this state can be seen throughout the Indian Subcontinent, especially near the tombs of the Sufis. They are referred to as, "Majzoobs". The Sufis glorify the insanity of the Majzoobs claiming that their state is not something that is acquired but something bestowed. Since apparently their 'intellect is overwhelmed by divine love' they are not liable for the Sharee'ah obligations. In other words the status of the "Majzoob" is just like an insane person whom the Sharee'ah is not applicable. Please note that Allah and His Messenger ﷺ are free from Majzoobs.

13

matters is participation in the jamaat (organization) activities - be it the 3-day outings, Fazaail-e-Aamaal reading sessions or the Ijtemaas (conferences).

The rest did not matter; whether it was correction of Aqeedah, seeking knowledge of the Deen, being sure of what you attribute to the Deen, the consequences of narrating those stories or dreams, evaluating the exaggerated claims of joining Tableeghi group's activities, etc.

As for us, these discussions chalked out guidelines for our research that we presented as advice to our Tableeghi brothers.

The first edition of the book,

The Jamaat Tableegh and the Deobandis.

A Critical analysis of their Beliefs, Books and Dawah

published in the year 2001

adhered to the following methodology...

- To base our analysis on textual evidences instead of evident flaws, and **highlight the harms that comes from stories of Fazaail-e-Aamaal.**

- To show that the **objectionable ideas are well-established Deobandi views** - approved and supported by the most authoritative Deobandi elders.

- We also took the added caution of **not attributing any peculiar opinion** of an individual Deobandi scholar to be the position of the Deobandis.

- To present proofs and quotations from the English translations of Deobandi books because these books have been published after the 1980's, and thus proving that **the Deobandis still adhere to these views,** and actively translate them for their newer audiences.

Experiences
from 2001-2011

The first edition of the book,

The Jamaat Tableegh and the Deobandis

A Critical analysis of their Beliefs, Books and Dawah

sold out within a year, and has been out of print since then. It is available online, where it has been downloaded in excess of 80,000 times.

The first edition was 300 pages, and **the second edition which is being worked upon is much larger and more authoritative** - as it has direct quotes and translations from major scholars of Ahlus-Sunnah.

This book is a concise version of the first edition, and we hope to publish the voluminous second edition in the near future, Insha'Allah.

A decade has passed since the publication of the first edition, and this has given us the opportunity to reflect, re-evaluate and further research our writings.

We have also received a lot of feedback, support and obviously hate-mail; and in them an observed pattern can be seen:

- Those who are aware of the Deobandi ideology never accused us of attributing incorrect views to the Deobandis. Rather they have sought to justify them.

- The general folk, who affiliate themselves to the Deobandis and actively participate in the Tableeghi Jamaat out of good intention, are largely unaware of the ideology that they are helping spread. And so, they out-rightly deny any connection with those beliefs; rather accuse us of making the Tableeghi Jamaat at par with the grave-worshiping group.

- And of course, there have been lots of people who have cross-checked our writings and referred back to the Deobandi scholars, and realized that the grave mistakes that were pointed out to, are indeed true without exaggeration or allegation.

So, we present this book to you in order that you reflect on the mistakes that have been pointed to in the Tableeghi Jamaat, and **not be deceived by exaggerated claims and misperceptions.** And that if you participate in any kind of dawah activity, then you do so out of an informed choice; well-aware of the consequences of the teachings that you are helping spread.

You do not want to enjoin good in a manner, which will result in a greater evil. **You do not want to teach a person the virtues of charity by narrating to him stories that give hope in benefitting from the dead - the foundation of grave-worship!** (see pg. 52-53)

We'd like to say that **this book is being presented to you purely out of concern and not out of hatred.** We have no personal enmity with the Deobandis or the Tableeghis - while a lot of our families come from this background.

But the truth has to be said, and one cannot remain a silent spectator while the people are given flawed teachings, and are being deprived of correct rectification in Aqeedah and action.

Tableeghi Jamaat and its relation to

Deoband and Sufism

Who are the Deobandis?

The term, Deobandi, is used to describe all those who follow the way of the Darul-Uloom Deoband, the institution founded by Moulana Qasim Nanotwi in 1868.

Qari Mohammed Tayyib (the director of the Darul-Uloom, Deoband) describes the Deobandis as,

"Religiously, the Ulama of Deoband are Muslims.

As a sect, they belong to the Ahlus-Sunnah wal-Jamaah.

By Madhhab they are Hanafee.

In conduct, they are Sufis.

Scholastically, they are Maturidi.

And in **Sulook, they are Chishti –**

rather they combine all Sufi orders

(Chishtiyyah, Naqshbandiya, Qadriyah and Soharwardiyah tareeqahs)[2]...

And in nisbat, they are Deobandi."

Mufti Abdur-Rahim Lajpuri in Fatawa Rahimiyyah,

(Eng. Trans.), vol.1, p.9-10 from Ulama-e-Deoband ka Maslak.

See. Also Muhannad alal-Mufannad p.29

The Tableeghi Jamaat is a Deobandi group

The Tableeghi Jamaat was founded by the Deobandi scholar, Moulana Muhammad Ilyas, who was much influenced by one of the most revered Deobandi elder, Moulana Ashraf Ali Thanvi.

Moulana Muhammad Ilyas used to say,

"Hazrat Moulana Ashraf Ali Thanvi has done a great service (to the religion). It is my heart's desire that the teachings should be his, and the Manhaj (methodology) of Dawah (propagation) be mine, so that in this way his teachings become well-known."

Malfoozat Moulana Ilyaas (Sayings of Moulana Ilyaas),

collected by Muhammad Manzoor Noomani, p.50, incident no. 56 (Urdu)

One can also refer to the official fatwa website of Darul-Uloom Deoband, where they explicitly declare that the Tableeghi Jamaat are Deobandis.

See. Darulifta-deoband.org (Fatwa website owned by Darul-Uloom Deoband)

(Fatwa: 519/521=M) and (Fatwa: 274/260=J)

---

[2] **Tareeqah and Sharee'ah**: According to the Soofis, Tareeqah is the way by which one reaches to Allah, and **Sharee'ah** is the path which reaches Jannah. Tareeqah is special and **Sharee'ah is common.** Tareeqah is based upon a particular set of beliefs, actions and exercises.
[A Dictionary of the Technical Terms used in the Sciences of the Musalmans
by Moulvi Muhammad Alee Ibn Alee Al-Thanvi, p 919]

Important
Personalities
amongst the Deobandis and the Tableeghi Jamaat

1. Imdadullah Muhajir Makki (d. 1899CE): The highly revered Pir (spiritual guide) of all the major Deobandi scholars. He is the spiritual guide of Moulana Ashraf Ali Thanvi, Moulana Qasim Nanotwi and Moulana Rasheed Ahmad Gangohi. He openly declared his belief in Wahdat al-Wajood[3] and promoted it in his writings.

2. Moulana Qasim Nanotwi (d. 1880CE): He founded Darul-Uloom Deoband in 1283H (1868 CE)[4] and was bayt (taken the oath of allegiance) at the hands of Imdadullah Muhajir Makki.[5]

3. Moulana Ashraf Ali Thanvi (d. 1943CE): He was bayt at the hands of Haji Imdadullah Muhajir Makki and the author of many books

---

[3] Wahdat al-Wujood is a concept based upon the idea that nothing exists other than Allah, and the creation is merely the manifestation of Allah.
[4] Mashaikh-e-Chist (Eng. Trans.) p.222
[5] Irshaadul-Mulook (Eng. Trans.) p.32

like, Bahishti Zewar and Tafseer Bayanul Qur'aan, that are used as reference works by the Deobandis. Like his Pir, Imdadullah Muhajir Makki, Moulana Ashraf Ali Thanvi too, was an advocate of Wahdat al-Wajood. His teachings greatly influenced the founder of the Tableeghi Jamaat, Moulana Ilyas - as mentioned earlier.

4. Rasheed Ahmad Gangohi (d. 1905CE): A prominent elder of the Deobandis, and close companion of Qasim Nanotwi. He too was bayt at the hands of Imdadullah Muhajir Makki[6]. From amongst his famous books is, 'Imdadus Sulook.'

5. Other Prominent Deobandi Scholars include:
- Khalil Ahmad Saharanpuri
  (author of Al-muhannad alal-mufannad),
- Moulana Aashiq Ilahi Meerathi,
- Moulana Mahmoodul-Hasan Deobandi,
- Moulana Shabbir Ahmad Uthmani,
- Moulana Abdul-Rahim Lajpuri and
- Moulana Husain Ahmed Madani.

Contemporary Deobandis include
- Mufti Taqi Uthmani,
- Maulana Hakeem Akhtar (the translator of Mathnawi),
- Mufti Yousuf Ludhyanvi and
- Moulana Sarfaraz Khan Safdar.

---

[6] Irshaadul-Mulook, (Eng. Trans.) p.32

6. Moulana Ilyas, popularly known as Hazratjee (1885CE -d. 1944CE): He was the **founder and first Amir** of the Tableeghi Jamaat. He was the Khalifah (successor) of Khalil Ahmad Saharanpuri, who was amongst the Khulafa of Rasheed Ahmad Gungohi.[7] He founded the Jamaat Tableegh on Sufi principles and incorporated many Sufi practices like Muraqabah (meditation), Chillah (40 day seclusion period) and the silent Dhikr (remembrance) into the routines of his Jamaat.

"**Bearing in mind the long soofee tradition amongst Muslims in India, Moulana Ilyas inaugurated a religious movement which aimed at reviving spiritual devotion by emphasizing soofee practices, which he adopted for his work with certain changes.**"[8]

7. Other Tableeghi Amirs:
Moulana Muhammad Yusuf (d.1965CE); Moulana Ilyas was succeeded by his son, Moulana Muhammad Yusuf, who became the second Amir of the Tableeghi Jamaat. He was succeeded by **Moulana Inamul-Hasan (d.1995CE)**. Presently, there is no one Amir, and the affairs of the Jamaat are run by a Shura (committee), which comprises of Moulana Saad Kandhalawi and Maulana Zubair ul-Hasan.[9]

8. Moulana Muhammad Zakariyah Kandhalwi (1898CE - 1982 CE): The son-in-law of Moulana Ilyas[10] and the author of Fazaail-e-Aamaal. He

---

[7] Irshaadul-Mulook, (Eng. Trans.) p.12.
[8] The Sufi Practices of Moulana Ilyas by M. Anwarul-Haqq, p. 37.
Awake, vol. 4, no. 10, March-April 1991, WMMA, South Africa.
[9] Times of India, Special-report, Tabligh-or-the-enigma-of-revival (2223665).
[10] Mashaikh-e-Chist (Eng. Trans.) p.307.

was well acquainted with Sufism and was given the Khilafah of all the four Sufi Tareeqahs by Moulana Khalil Ahmad Saharanpuri.[11]

---

[11] Mashaikh-e-Chist (Eng. Trans.) p.304-305.

The Tableeghi Jamaat's
Handbook

Originally known as Tableeghi Nisaab, 'Fazaail-e-Aamaal' literally means the virtues (Fazaail) of acts of worship (Aamaal).

It consists of a series of booklets written by Moulana Zakariyyah Kandhalvi on the instructions of Moulana Ilyas (the founder of Tableeghi Jamaat) as mentioned by Moulana Zakariyyah himself in his autobiography, 'Aap Beeti'.

Fazaail-e-Aamaal consists of nine booklets, namely
Hikayaat Sahabah,   Fazaail-e-Dhikr,
Fazaail-e-Namaaz,   Fazaail-e-Tableegh,
Fazaail-e-Qur'aan,   Fazaail-e-Darood,
Fazaail-e-Ramadaan,   Fazaail-e-Sadaqat
and Fazaail-e-Hajj.

These series were compiled in two volumes and entitled, 'Tableeghi Nisaab.' They were intended to be the handbook of the Tableeghi Jamaat.

Later on, it was re-named, 'Fazaail-e-Aamaal.' This book originally in Urdu, has been translated to many different languages.

The Definition and Reality of

Sufism

The Deobandis attribute themselves to Sufism, and assert that Sufism is just another name for Tazkeyyatun-Nafs (purification of the self) and Ihsan (the highest stage of Eemaan).

Moulana Muhammad Maseehullah Khan, a Khalifah (successor) of Moulana Ashraf Alee Thanvi states,

"It's (Sufism) function is to purify the heart from the lowly bestial attributes of lust, calamities of the tongue, anger, malice, jealousy, love of this world, love for fame, niggardliness, greed, vanity, deception, etc." [Shariat and Tasawwuf, p.11]

And, as such, they claim that Sufism does not contradict the Sharee'ah (Islamic Regulation), rather they say,

"It is incumbent for every Muslim to become a Sufi. Without Sufism, a Muslim cannot be described as a perfect Muslim." [Shariat and Tasawwuf, p.11]

In reality however, Sufism is much more than purification of the self; for, self-purification is part of the religion of Islam and it has been completely explained by Allah's Messenger 〓.

"Purification of the Soul" as Moulana Muhammad Maseehullah Khan explains, is just the first part of the journey of Sufism, and it is referred as a journey towards Allah. [See, Shariat and Tasawwuf p.112]

The next part of this journey is called, 'Journey into Allah', and

"In this high stage of spiritual development, matters pertaining to the Thaat (Being of Allah), Sifaat (Attributes of Allah), Af'aal (Acts of Allah), Haqaaiq (realities) as well as relationships between Allah and His servants become manifest."

Shariat and Tasawwuf p.113

And thus, everything is manifest to the Sufis and nothing is hidden from them. They claim to accomplish this by either exaggerating in prescribed forms of worship, or indulging in innovative forms of worship. This is Sufism.

Attachment to

graves

is persistently

endorsed

in the stories of

Fazaail-e-Aamaal

The following are some stories from Fazaail-e-Aamaal
that mention **calling upon** the Messenger of Allah ﷺ.

1. From Fazaail-e-Aamaal (Virtues of Hajj) (abridged):

A traveler relates, "At the grave of Rasulullah I said, 'I have come
from Egypt and for five months now, I have been in your presence.

I beg of Allah and of you that one such person should take
charge of feeding me so that I become able to depart homewards from

here.' Thereafter, I prayed for further things, went and sat down near the Minbar (pulpit).

A man then came to him and gave him food... After the hungry man had eaten to his fill, he was given the remaining food in a basket...

The man (who fed the traveler) then said, '**By Allah, do not ever complain to my grandfather, Rasoolullah again**. It disturbs him greatly...' He then sent a servant along with the traveler to reach him to the Prophet's grave.

Upon reaching Baqi, the traveler said to the servant, "It is all right, for now I know the way. You may return." The slave replied, "I have not the right to return without having left you at the grave. Perhaps, Rasoolullah will inform my master if I should."

Fazaail-e-Aamaal, (Eng. Trans.), Virtues of Hajj,
Chapter. 9, p.180, story no.28,
(New Edition 1982, Published by Dini Book Depot - Delhi)

2. From Fazaail-e-Aamaal (Virtues of Hajj):

"Hazrat Ibn Jalaa relates, "While in Medina, I once suffered tremendous hunger. It became so unbearable that I presented myself at the grave of Rasoolullah and said, "**O Rasoolullah, I suffer great hunger. I am now your guest.**"

Thereafter, sleep overtook me and in a vision, I saw Rasoolullah gave me a piece of bread. I ate half of it and when I woke up, I found myself with the other half of that piece of bread still in my hands."

Fazaail-e-Aamaal, (Eng. Trans.), Virtues of Hajj
Chapter.9, p.178, story no.23, (New Edition 1982, Published by Dini Book Depot - Delhi)
Similar incidents have been mentioned on p.171 (story no.8)

3. From Fazaail-e-Aamaal (Virtues of Hajj):

"In Medina, there lived a woman from the Hashimi family, whose servants used to ill-treat her. **She went with her complaints to Rasoolullah where she poured out her heart.**

From the grave was heard this reply, "Do you not prefer to follow my excellent example. Have patience, as I patiently persevered."

She said, "After hearing that voice all my grief disappeared, and all the servants who used to annoy me passed away."

Fazaail-e-Aamaal, (Eng. Trans.), Virtues of Hajj,
Chapter.9, p.175, story no.16,
(New Edition 1982, Published by Dini Book Depot - Delhi)

4. From Fazaail-e-Aamaal (Virtues of Hajj) (abridged):

Three men fasted for days on end since they could not find food. **One of them went to the grave of Rasoolullah and said, "O Rasoolullah, hunger has overtaken us."**

Soon afterwards ... "a man from Alawi family knocked at the door. We opened the door and found a man with two servants, each one carrying a large basket with many delicious foods."

The man from the Alawi family said before leaving, "You have complained about hunger to Rasoolullah. I have seen Rasoolullah in a dream and he commanded me to bring food to you."

Fazaail-e-Aamaal, (Eng. Trans.), Virtues of Hajj,
Chapter.9, p.177, story no.22, (New Edition 1982. Published by Dini Book Depot - Delhi).
Similar stories have been mentioned on p.179 (story no.27) and p.181 (story no.29)

5. From Fazaail-e-Aamaal (Virtues of Hajj) (abridged):

Once a Muazzin was giving Adhaan (the call of prayer) when someone came along and struck him a hard smack. Crying, the Muazzin said,

"... O Rasoolullah! See what is done to me in your esteemed presence!"

Immediately after the complaint, the (attacking) person was paralyzed and fell down. People who were nearby picked him up and took him home, where after three days he died."

Fazaail-e-Aamaal, (Eng. Trans.), Virtues of Hajj,
Chapter.9, story no.26, p.179,
(New Edition 1982, Published by Dini Book Depot - Delhi)

6. In one story, a man named Abu Muhammad had to repay 80 gold coins that were kept as a trust with him. He spent the money and had no one who could help him repay.

So he ... **"...then went to the grave of Rasoolullah, where he made Du'aa for the whole night, sometimes at the grave and sometime at the minbar (pulpit), begging for a way out of his predicament.**

In the latter part of the night, he heard a voice coming to him from the darkness near the grave saying, 'O Abu Muhammad, take this.' My father stretched forth his hand and a bag was given to him. In it were 80 gold coins!"

Fazaail-e-Aamaal, (Eng. Trans.), Virtues of Hajj
Chapter.9, p.177, story no.21,
(New Edition 1982, Published by Dini Book Depot - Delhi).
A similar story is mentioned on p.178 (story no.24)

What do these stories teach the reader?

Should such stories be circulated amongst common Muslims?

As is clear to any reader - **not only do these stories of Fazaail-e-Aamaal clearly endorse calling upon the Prophet ﷺ after his death for help, but** they also inform that help is actually received when someone calls upon the Prophet ﷺ near his grave!!

One should know clearly that any form of calling upon (i.e. Dua to) the dead - including calling upon the Prophet ﷺ after his death, is Shirk (associating partners with Allah).

"Invoke not besides Allah, any such that will neither profit you nor harm you, but if (in case) you did so, you shall certainly be one of the Zalimun (polytheist and wrong-doers)."

[Soorah Yunus (10): 106]

Fazaail-e-Aamaal's stories thus, pose a great danger to the vulnerable Aqeedah (creed, faith) of general Muslims. This is especially so because those who read and hear these stories are never taught Tawheed as it should be, and what nullifies it.

Yet, such stories continue to be circulated irresponsibly amongst the masses, which is in contrast to the way of Allah's Messenger ﷺ, who showed much keenness towards protecting the Aqeedah (belief, faith) of the Muslims, and **he ﷺ severely warned against performing any form of worship near graves, especially the graves of the Prophets.**

The wisdom behind this prohibition was to exterminate the very root of Shirk - i.e., calling upon the dead for help. By prohibiting any form of worship (whether Salaat or dua for oneself) near the graves, the Prophet ﷺ closed the door for Shaytaan to misguide his ﷺ Ummah (nation) into committing the Shirk of worshiping (calling upon) the dead.

It would have been easy for the Shaytaan to fool those worshiping Allah at the graves, into worshiping the dead buried in those graves - just like he deceived the people of Nuh (عليه السلام) into committing Shirk by first convincing them to erect idols in their places of worship, and then eventually causing the later generations to worship those idols.[12]

---

[12] Imam Ibnil-Qayyim (رحمه الله) said,

"There are several ways in which Shaytaan fooled the Mushrikeen into idol-worship; he played with every nation in accordance with their mind-set and way of thinking.

He invited some people to idol-worship through honoring the dead. These people sculptured idols in the shape of the righteous as had occurred with the people of Nuh (عليه سلام). This is why Allah's Messenger ﷺ has cursed those who make mosques on graves and he forbade Salaat at graves." [Igathatul-Afhaan, (2/222-223)]

An important Additional
Clarification

One Argument that is often brought up in defense of Fazaail-e-Aamaal is that **Moulana Zakariyyah did not invent these stories, and these can be found in books from the past.**

Reply: Scholars might include something in their books merely for historical record, or to refute it or they might include a story with its isnad (chain of narration) so that other scholars can know its authenticity from it. So, if a story is found in the book of a particular scholar,

- **it does not necessarily mean that the scholar finds it acceptable** or that he has established its authenticity,
- and more importantly, **it does not mean that the author necessarily wants to teach you your Aqeedah from that story.**

Now, this reply is also given by those who defend Fazaail-e-Aamaal. They say **these stories are not to teach Aqeedah but merely to encourage righteous actions.**

Reply:

1. There is a big difference between a scholar recording a story in his voluminous book, and someone collecting all such stories from various voluminous books and compiling them together.

There is a big difference between recording a story in a book meant to be read by scholars, and a collection of such stories being presented to the ignorant commoner, who the Tableeghi brothers themselves describe as 'being unaware of even the kalimah.'

There is a big difference between recording a story in a book that has in it clarification about the correct Aqeedah, and between a book with an entire chapter of such stories **without clarification**, where the ignorant commoner is left to his own understanding.

And it must be kept in mind that our environment is one where ignorance, superstitions and ideas of shirk are prevalent.

2. The argument that these stories are to encourage righteous actions and not to teach Aqeedah would carry weight if the Aqeedah of the author was in reality, different from the falsehood present in these stories.

For example, Moulana Zakariyyah, the author of Fazaail-e-Aamal, has quoted Haji Imdadullah Muhajir Makki (the most respected peer of the Deobandis) in Mashaikh-e-Chist,

"...The Faqir does not die. He is simply transformed from one abode to another. **The same benefit which was received from the Faqir's physical life will be acquired from his grave.**"

Mashaikh-e-Chist (Eng. Trans.) p.211

So if this is the Aqeedah approved by Moulana Zakariyyah, who has collected the stories that give the message that the dead benefit the living - **then on what basis can one argue that the intent is to encourage actions, and not to teach the false Aqeedah endorsed in it?**

Such an argument is only justified for those who warn against those false beliefs and ideas, and also clarify those beliefs as unacceptable mistakes - while at the same time respect a particular book for the benefit in it. (also, see pg. 57)

3. Enjoining good cannot be done in a manner that will result in a greater evil. One cannot spread a story that encourages generosity, if the same story endorses false beliefs like the dead is aware of the world, and continues to benefit the living after his death. (also, see pg. 52-53)

Moreover, these stories do not comprise of essential Islamic knowledge that a common person needs to know, and cannot do without. Rather the opposite is true. These stories have in them that which corrupts the Aqeedah.

There is enough in the Qur'aan and the Sunnah to encourage righteous actions as can be found in Fazaail-e-Aamal itself. So, **why is there a need for such stories,** except to those who wish for people to have a 'sufi-vision' of Islam.

4. Even this argument that, "these stories are not to teach Aqeedah but merely to encourage righteous actions", is not mentioned/clarified in Tableeghi circles, but only brought up as a reply to the critics of Tableeghi Jamaat!

The Prophet ﷺ severely

warned against

taking graves as places of worship
even on his death-bed!

وروى مسلم في (الجنائز 970) صحيحه عن جندب بن عبد الله البجلي

قال سمعت رسول الله صلى الله عليه وسلم يقول:

" ... أَلا وإنّ من كان قبلكم كانوا يتخذون قبور أنبيائهم وصالحيهم

مساجد أَلا فلا تتخذوا القبور مساجد إني أنهاكم عن ذلك."

Imam Muslim narrated in his Saheeh that
Jundub ibn Abdillaah al-Bajali said that he heard the Messenger of Allah ﷺ
say:

> "...Those who came before you took the graves of their Prophets and
> righteous people as places of worship. **Do not take graves as**
> **Masaajid (sing. Masjid- i.e., place of worship) for, I forbid you to**
> **do that."** Saheeh Muslim, al-Janaa'iz, (970)

"إن من شرار الناس من تدركهم الساعة وهم أحياء،
والذين يتخذون القبور مساجد."

أخرجه أحمد (1/405) وأصله في البخاري معلقاً : كتاب الفتن ، باب ظهور الفتن (7076)

Allah's Messenger ﷺ said,

"The most evil of people are those upon whom the Hour will come
when they are still alive and **those who take graves as places of
worship.**"

Narrated by Imaam Ahmad (1/405). It is also narrated by al-Bukharee in a
mu'allaq report in Kitaab al-Fitan, Baab Zuhoor al-Fitan (7067).

حدثني يحيى بن بُكير: حدثنا الليث، عن عُقَيل، عن ابن شهاب قال :أخبرني عبيد الله بن عبد الله بن عتبة: أن
عائشة وعبد الله بن عباس رضي الله عنهم قالا:

"لما نزل برسول الله صلى الله عليه وسلم، طفق يطرح خميصة له على
وجهه، فإذا اغتم كشفها عن وجهه، فقال وهو كذلك: "لعنة الله على اليهود
والنصارى، اتخذوا قبور أنبيائهم مساجد." يُحَذِّر ما صنعوا.

صحيح البخاري -كتاب اللباس (18) باب: الأكسية والخمائص (5478)

Narrated Aisha and Abdullah bin Abbas (رضى الله عنهم),

"When the last moment of the life of Allah's Messenger ﷺ came, he
started putting his 'Khamisa' (cloth) on his face, and when he felt hot
and short of breath he took it off his face and said, '**May Allah curse
the Jews and Christians for they built places of worship at the
graves of their Prophets.**'"

(Aisha and Abdullah bin Abbas added),

"The Prophet ﷺ was warning (the Muslims) of what they had done."

Saheeh al-Bukharee, Book no. 8, Hadeeth no. 427
Also see, Saheeh al-Bukharee, Book. no.18 The Book of Dress

عن عائشة رضي الله عنها أنها قالت:

"لما نزل برسول الله صلى الله عليه وسلم طفق يطرح خميصة له على وجهه فإذا اغتم بها كشفها، فقال وهو كذلك: لعنة الله على ليهود والنصارى اتخذوا قبور أنبيائهم مساجد، يحذّر ما صنعوا، **ولولا ذلك أبرز قبره غير أنه** خشي أن يتخذ مسجدًا."

رواه البخاري ومسلم

Aisha added, (after narrating the above narration),

"…Had it not been so, his (the Prophet's ﷺ) grave would have been in an open place, but it could not be due to the fear that it may be taken as a mosque."

Saheeh Muslim, Book of Salaat (04), Hadeeth no. 1079

These Ahaadeeth are proof that the accursed ones are those who take the graves as a masjid (mosque), and **Masjid is a place where Dua is made to Allah** (سبحانه و تعالى).

﴿وَأَنَّ الْمَسَاجِدَ لِلَّهِ فَلاَ تَدْعُواْ مَعَ اللَّهِ أَحَداً﴾

"The mosques are for Allah (Alone),
so invoke not anyone along with Allah."

[Soorah al-Jinn (72):18]

Salaat itself is the greatest form of Dua
and 'Salaat' means 'Dua' in the arabic language.
Allah (سبحانه و تعالى) says,

﴿خُذْ مِنْ أَمْوَلِهِمْ صَدَقَةً تُطَهِّرُهُمْ وَتُزَكِّيهِم بِهَا
وَصَلِّ عَلَيْهِمْ إِنَّ صَلَوَتَكَ سَكَنٌ لَّهُمْ﴾

"Take Sadaqah (charity) from their wealth
in order to purify them and sanctify them with it,
and invoke (وَصَلِّ) for them.
Verily! Your invocations (صَلَوَتَكَ)
are a source of security for them."
[Soorah at-Tawbah (9): 103]

So, if masjids are for the purpose of Dua to Allah to be done in them, and the curse of Allah is upon the one who takes the graves as masajid then this means:

- **Serious and Severe Prohibition** of taking graves as places of Dua (to Allah for oneself) and
- **Severe rejection** of the one who makes Dua (for himself) around it.

And if this is the case of the one who makes Dua near the grave, but invokes Allah Alone for his needs - **So what would be said about those who call upon the dead for their needs?!**

It is imperative for the Muslims to ponder upon the fact that Allah's Messenger ﷺ was someone who detested vain talk and only spoke based upon revelation. And, when he ﷺ warned against taking graves as places of

---

41

worship, he was on his death-bed - when even common people do not speak of insignificant matters.

The situation (i.e., death-bed) and the curse - show that **Allah's Messenger** ﷺ **was warning against something that is a real and serious danger upon the Muslim nation,** which is their falling into the same mistake as the Jews and Christians - i.e., taking graves as places of worship.

It also shows the Prophet's ﷺ keenness to protect his Ummah (nation) from all forms of Shirk, especially those related to the dead to the extent that **visiting graves was absolutely forbidden in the early years of Islam** in order to prevent the graves from becoming mediums of Shirk.

Visiting graves was only made permissible after Tawheed (making all worship for Allah Alone) was firmly established in the hearts of the Sahabah (رضى الله عنهم).

Allah's Messenger ﷺ said,

"I used to forbid you from visiting graves,

but now you should visit them -

for, surely they are reminders of the next life."

Saheeh Muslim (Eng. Trans.) vol.2, p.463-464, no.2131

(and in another narration),

"So whoever wishes to visit (the graves) may do so, but don't say Hujr (i.e., obscenity/falsehood at the graves)."

This addition is found in an-Nasa'ee (2033)
Classed as saheeh by al-Albanee in as-Silsilah as-Saheehah (886)

Allamah Ibnil-Qayyim (رحمه الله) said,

"Allah's Messenger ﷺ had prohibited the men from visiting the graves so as to prevent it (the graves) from becoming a medium (of Shirk).

So, when the Tawheed (worship for Allah Alone) was established in their hearts, he ﷺ permitted them to visit the graves in the manner he ﷺ prescribed - and he forbade them from saying Hujr (i.e., obscenity/falsehood at the graves).

So anyone who visited it (the graves, in a way) different from that which was prescribed; the way that is loved by Allah and His Messenger, then his visiting the grave[13] is not permitted (i.e., unacceptable); **and from the greatest Hujr is Shirk in words and actions.**" Igathatul-Lahfan (1/218)

---

[13] The prescribed form of Ziyarah is that the person visits a common graveyard (without journeying to specific tombs) with the intention of:

a) Remembering death
b) Dua (supplicating) for the engraved in the prescribed way, 'Peace be upon the Believers and Muslims among the inhabitants of these dwellings. May Allah have mercy on those who have gone ahead of us, and those following us. And we shall, Allah-willing, be joining you.' [Saheeh Muslim (Eng. Trans.) vol.2, p.461-2, no.2127]

The innovated form of Ziyarah is that which contradicts the prescribed form of Ziyarah, like
a) Visiting the grave for seeking help from the engraved,
b) Visiting the graves with the intention of making Dua for oneself or any other form of worship at the grave believing that the worship is more acceptable near the grave, like formal prayers, reciting the Qur'aan, sacrifice, etc. because this would amount to making graves a place of worship.

To further illustrate how the Fazail-Aamal promotes
Hujr (i.e., obscenity/falsehood)
and undue veneration of graves ...

Undue
Veneration of the graves
in the stories of Fazaail-e-Aamaal

Story endorsing that Dua (supplication)
is more acceptable near graves

Moulana Zakariyyah mentions a story of two brothers whose father
died leaving behind an inheritance, which included three strands of
hair of Allah's Messenger ﷺ.

The brothers divided the property in half, so that they had one
strand of hair each. They, however, disputed about the third strand of
hair.

The elder brother agreed to give the younger brother all the three strands of hair, if the younger parted off with his share of the property, to which the younger brother happily agreed.

When the younger brother died, "...many pious people dreamt of the Holy Prophet, who told them, 'If a person has any need he should ask it from Allah sitting at the side of his grave.'"

Fazaail-e-Aamaal, (Eng. Trans.) Virtues of Darood, Chapter.5, story no.35, p.128. (Edition 1985, Published by Dini Book Depot - Delhi)

The idea that Dua (supplication) is more acceptable near graves is what has given rise to the practice of regular visits to certain tombs for the purpose of prayer and Dua, and we have seen already the serious prohibition of taking the graves as places of worship.

Furthermore, how can someone allege that Allah's Messenger ﷺ directed the people to a grave as a place for Dua, when he ﷺ opposed taking graves as places for worship, and cursed the Jews and Christians for this action!!!

Asking the Prophet for
Shafa'ah is endorsed
in the stories of Fazaail-e-Aamaal

Despite the presence of stories in Fazaail-e-Aamaal that mention calling upon the engraved or imploring at graves, the Deobandis openly declare that calling upon the dead is Shirk[14] - But this declaration of theirs is seriously blemished by their approval and encouragement of asking the Prophet ﷺ for intercession (Shafa'ah) after his death at his grave-side.

In Fazaail-e-Hajj (Virtues of Hajj) under, 'The Manner of performing Ziyaarat', Moulana Zakariyyah encourages the visitors to the grave of Allah's Messenger ﷺ to request the Prophet ﷺ for intercession (i.e., to make Dua to Allah on one's behalf) for forgiveness of sins, he writes:

---

[14] For instance, it is mentioned in Kitabul-Janaiz p.21-24,
  "The Islamic meaning of Waseelah does not consist of praying or making Dua to Rasoolullah or any other created being.
  Islam teaches that the only Being to whom prayers and Dua have to be directed is Allah. Directing one's prayer and Dua to any being other than Allah is Shirk or polytheism, and Shirk is the worst of sins committed against Allah."

"...we have the following Dua to be recited together with the salutation at the grave of the Nabi Sal'am,

"... ... now have I come to you O Rasul,
seeking forgiveness for my sins,
Seeking your intercession on my behalf
in the presence of Allah..."

Fazaail-e-Aamaal, (Eng. Trans.), Virtues of Hajj, Chapter.9, pg.151, point.32, (New Edition 1982, Published by Dini Book Depot - Delhi)

Other similar mentions can be found in the chapter of, 'The Manner of Ziyarah'. It is beyond the scope of this book to present extensive quotes from the authoritative books of the Deobandis concerning Shafa'ah, and reply to all their arguments in detail.[15]

So, we suffice here by mentioning the basic and clear arguments that falsify the idea of asking intercession from the Prophet 🕌 after his death.

- The Prophet 🕌 was the most-merciful to his ummah, and thus, whenever someone requested him to make Dua during his lifetime, he 🕌 never refused, and he 🕌 would always make Dua on behalf of the Muslims.

  So, if he 🕌 was capable to make Dua on behalf of the Muslims forever, even after his 🕌 death, then **why did the Prophet 🕌 prohibit taking his grave as a place of worship? And why did he curse those who took the graves of their Prophets, as places of worship?**

---

[15] Read a detailed analysis of the arguments and proofs of the Deobandis in defense of Shafa'ah including,
- the story of al-A'rabi,
- the narration of Malik ad-Dar,
- ayah 64 of Soorah an-Nisa

and more in the second edition of the book,
The Jamaat Tableegh and the Deobandis
soon to be published by Quran Sunnah Education Programs.
Insha'Allah, the book will also be made available online for free download at www.qsep.com

- If it was permissible to ask the Prophet ﷺ to make Dua on one's behalf after his ﷺ death, the Prophet ﷺ would himself encourage the Muslims to come to his grave, and request his intercession **but there is no Hadeeth in this regard!!**

- What further falsifies the practice of asking intercession from the dead, is that **seeking intercession from the dead was the very Shirk of the pagan Arabs**, whom Allah's Messenger ﷺ fought against.

  The Arab pagans invoked the dead righteous and the dead prophets, and their argument was that the righteous dead are our intercessors with Allah.

  Allah (سبحانه و تعالى) said about them, "They worship besides Allah things that harm them not, nor profit them, and they say, "These are our intercessors with Allah." [Soorah Yunus (10): 18]

- **Asking Shafa'ah from the dead is Shirk** because the Qur'aan denies asking Shafaah (intercession) from anyone other than Allah.

$$﴿أَم اتَّخَذُواْ مِن دُونِ اللَّهِ شُفَعَآءَ قُلْ أَوَلَوْ كَانُواْ لاَ يَمْلِكُونَ شَيْئًا وَلاَ يَعْقِلُونَ - قُل لِّلَّهِ الشَّفَعَةُ جَمِيعًا﴾$$

**"Have they taken others as intercessors besides Allah?...
Say, 'To Allah belongs all intercession..'"**

[Soorah az-Zumar (39): 43-44]

It is true that on the Day of Judgment, some of the creation of Allah like, His Prophets, His righteous slaves, and others will intercede for the people, but these intercessions will take place with two conditions;

- They will intercede only after **Allah has given them permission to intercede**, and
- They will only intercede on behalf of those **whom Allah is pleased with.**

and these two conditions are mentioned in the Qur'aan:

$$﴿مَن ذَا الَّذِى يَشْفَعُ عِندَهُ إِلاَّ بِإِذْنِهِ﴾$$

"Who is he that can intercede with Him
(i.e., Allah) except with His Permission?"

[Soorah al-Baqarah (2): 255]

$$﴿وَلاَ يَشْفَعُونَ إِلاَّ لِمَنِ ارْتَضَى﴾$$

"...they cannot intercede except for him
with whom He (i.e., Allah) is pleased..."

[Soorah al-Ambiya (21): 28-29]

Even in this worldly life, **if intercession is sought from Allah without His Permission and Pleasure, then the Shafa'ah is not accepted**, like the Shafa'ah of Prophet Nuh (عليه سلام) on behalf of his son, and Prophet Ibraheem (عليه سلام) on behalf of his father, and of our Prophet Muhammad ﷺ on behalf of his uncle.

The reason and wisdom behind this condition (of Allah's Permission and Pleasure) **is that everybody should turn to Allah, and not attach himself to others beside Him for Shafa'ah.**

So, **if intercession is sought, then it should be sought from Allah alone**, like saying, "O Allah, grant us the Shafa'ah of Allah's Messenger 🕌 and do not deprive us from this Shafa'ah..."

Moreover, it should be understood that **Shafa'ah is only a pretext by which Allah forgives his sinful slaves, and an honor which Allah bestows upon His righteous slaves.** And the greatest honor is granted to Prophet Muhammad 🕌, who informed us that he 🕌 is the first intercessor.

"Abu Hurayrah reported Allah's Messenger 🕌 saying,
'I shall be pre-eminent amongst the descendants of Adam
on the Day of Resurrection and I will be the first intercessor and the
first whose intercession will be accepted (by Allah).'"

Saheeh Muslim (30/5655)

- This saying of the Prophet 🕌, "the first intercessor" means absolute precedence without exception - precedence over everybody.

  Those who claim that the Prophet 🕌 intercedes after his death in his grave, and the righteous also intercede after their death, **then they should be asked the meaning of the Prophet's 🕌 statement, "I am the first intercessor".**

- If the Prophet 🕌 intercedes in his grave - then (this means that) he intercedes from the time of his death until the trumpet will be blown - and therefore, there is no meaning to the words, 'I am the first intercessor.'

If he were to intercede in his grave, then this superiority of the Day of Judgment in being the first intercessor is non-existent!

- If the Prophet ﷺ interceded during his lifetime by making Dua, and he intercedes after his death, and then he will intercede after the establishment of the Day of Resurrection - then what is the meaning of, 'I am the first intercessor.'

In this case, he is an intercessor all the time and his intercession is always accepted according to these claimants. **If it was so, then what is benefit of the Prophet informing us that he ﷺ is the first intercessor and the first one, whose intercession is accepted?**

Fazaail-e-Aamaal contains stories of

complaining at the graves,

and the dead performing righteous actions
that benefit the living!!

From Fazaail-e-Aamaal (Virtues of Charity) (abridged):

A virtuous man once sat down near the grave of a generous person and related that he needed some Deenaars (money) to help a beggar. In the night, he saw the man of the grave in his dream, who directed the virtuous man to go to his house where in a corner lay buried five hundred Deenaars, which he should give it to the beggar.

Next morning, the man visited the house of the man in the grave, spoke to the family members and thus, the Deenaars were found.

The man told the family members to keep the wealth for they were legal successors of the wealth. But they refused saying that it was shameful for them that their ancestor could be generous even after his death and they could not be during their life. The Deenars were thus, given to the beggar but the beggar only took half a Deenar.

See, Fazaail-e-Aamaal, (Eng. Trans.), Virtues of Charity,
Chapter.7, story no.24, p.195-196

There is no clarification, before or after this story that such-and-such belief is not true, and that this story is only meant to encourage charity. Instead, what is found is the following **comment by Moulana Zakariyyah**,

"The thing to be noted and considered in the above story is as to who was most generous? The deceased or his family or the beggar?

In our view, the beggar was most generous as in spite of his needs, he did not take more than half of a Deenar." [end quote]

Can a just person, after reading this comment, honestly say that a commoner to whom such stories are read, will only take encouragement for righteous actions from it, and not form a misguided opinion about the ability of the dead righteous to perform righteous acts and benefit the living? Rather, **this story helps formulate the belief, and Moulana Zakariyyah's comment re-enforces it!**

The idea that benefits may be received from the grave is the basic premise for grave worship. And we have seen already the dangers of attachment to graves, and the severe warning by Allah's Messenger 🕌 against taking graves as places of worship.

As for the intent of Moulana Zakariyyah, none can argue, after reading his comment, that such stories are not meant to teach a particular Aqeedah, especially since he himself approves,

"The same benefit which was received from the Faqir's physical life will be acquired from his grave."

Mashaikh-e-Chist (Eng. Trans.) p.211

The unanimous

Aqeedah of the Deobandis

and their approval of
benefiting from the graves

From Aqaaid Ahlus-Sunnah wal-Jamaa'at

(a Summary of Aqaaid Ulamaa-e-Deoband / Muhannad alal Mufannad),

by Moulana Mufti Syed Abdush-Shakoor Tirmidhi,

Published by Idarah Islamiyaat, Lahore, Pakistan, p.173

"Aqeedah no. 24: To benefit from the spirituality of the Mashaikh (and elders) and **to benefit from the hearts and graves is undoubtedly correct,** but in a way that is known to its bearers and experts and not on the way that is wide-spread amongst the people."

This book, Muhannad alal-Mufannad, was written to clarify the positions and Aqaaid (beliefs) of the Deobandis, after they were complained about to the scholars of Medina during the Turkish rule.

Moulana Khaleed Ahmed Saharanpuri wrote a reply to 26 questions raised, and got them approved by

- Moulana Mahmood ul-Hassan Deobandi,
- Moulana Ahmed Hassan Amrohi,
- Moulana Shah Abur-Raheem Raipuri,
- Moulana Ashraf Alee Thanwi, and
- Mufti Muhammad Kifatullah Dehlwi.

As the book states,

"… this collection (of questions and answers) was compiled in 1325H, and it is **not** that the beliefs mentioned in this book **are merely the beliefs of an individual, nor should they be considered as unreal and un-researched answers that were merely written as a temporary response to the people of innovation …**

rather these answers were a response to the questions raised by the scholars of Medina and were presented as researched beliefs of the elders of Deoband and that too **on behalf of the Jamaat of Deoband.**

Therefore **this collection is a written and unanimous document for knowing the collective beliefs of the scholars of Deoband …** and this is also a response to the one who falsely attributes any type of belief to the scholars of Deoband."

An incident recorded by Moulana Ashraf Alee Thanwi on how people benefited from the grave of a Deobandi elder.

From Arwah-e-Salasa, pg. 257, point no. 363:

"Moulvi Moin ud-Deen, who was the eldest son of Moulana Muhammad Ya'qoub, used to mention a Karamah (which occurred after death), that once in our Nanota, there was an outbreak of fever. **So, whosoever would tie the mud of the grave of Moulana (Muhammad Ya'qoub), would be cured only.** So, they would take the mud so frequently that whenever I would put more mud, it would finish. The mud was put many times.

Annoyed, this young man was very short tempered, once he went to the grave of Moulana and said **"For you, it is a karamat (miracle) and for us it is a problem. Beware that if this time anyone gets cured, then we will not fill your grave with mud.** Stay as you are. People will walk on you with their shoes."

So, from that day onwards no one was relieved. And as the news of cure had spread, the news that it (the mud of the grave) no longer cures, spread. And then, the people stopped taking the mud."

Conclusion

The environment we are in, and the prevalence of grave-worship, ignorance and misunderstandings, necessitates that people are given the pure message of Tawheed, such that it frees them from the clutches of shirk and superstitions; and that the people are repulsed more by shirk than by swine meat.

Their understanding of Tawheed should save them from clear and apparent shirk like calling upon other than Allah, as well as from more subtle forms, like turning to amulets sold at tombs for cure.

This however, will not be achieved under the patronage of the Tableeghi Jamaat that relies on misguided stories for relaying its message, and cannot free itself from its baggage of Sufism, and all the superstitions that go with it.

At the very least, those who associate with this Jamaat will fail to understand the gravity of shirk, and amongst other essential matters, the dangers of attachment to, and veneration of graves.

Ponder upon the concern of Allah's Messenger ﷺ in warning against the shirk that originates from veneration of graves, and compare that with the laxity and indifference shown on the matter in the Fazaail-e-Aamaal.

If you understand that the priority and the most important aspect of Islaah (reformation) in the lives of Muslims is their being upon the correct Aqeedah, then you should know that the Tableeghi Jamaat is not the group that will bring about this Islaah.

"I only desire reform to the best of my power.

And my guidance cannot come except from Allah,

in Him I trust and unto Him I repent."
[Soorah Hud (11): 88]

Appendix:
The reality of

Unusual Activities

near graves and tombs

by Shaikhul-Islam ibn Taymiyyah (رحمه الله)
from the book, 'Qaidah Jalilah' paragraph no. 95-142

Translated by Shawana A. Aziz

There is no doubt that there occurs hearing of voices and (unusual) activities near idols from the Shaytaan and this is one of the causes behind the misguidance of the children of Adam.

Making graves an idol was the first Shirk, and therefore some people hear voices, see men or strange incidents near the graves - **these (unusual incidents) are thought to be from the dead while they might be from the Jinn and Shayateen** (pl. of Shaytaan). For example, one sees that the grave breaks open and the dead rises up from it, speaks to him and hugs him - this is seen at the graves of the Prophets and others. But verily it is the Shaytaan, who takes the shape of mankind and falsely calls himself such and such Prophet or Shaykh. There are too many incidents in this regard to mention here.

The ignorant thinks that what he sees - that the one who came out of the grave, and hugged him and spoke to him - is the dead person buried in the grave or the Prophet or the righteous, etc., (but) **the believer knows that it is a Shaytaan** and this can be shown by many ways:

a) **Sincerely Reciting the Ayat al-Kursi**. The man will disappear, go back into the earth or hide when Aayat al-Kursi is recited. If he were a righteous man or an angel, or a believing jinn then Aayat al-Kursi would not have harmed him. It only harms the Shayateen as is established in the Saheeh from the hadeeth of Abu Hurayrah(رضى الله عنه) when the Jinn told him, "When you go to your bed, recite Aayat al-Kursi, and you will have ongoing protection from Allah and no Shaytaan will come near you until morning comes." The Prophet ﷺ said, "He spoke the truth even though he is a liar."

[Saheeh al-Bukharee (3101)]

b) **Seeking Refuge with Allah from the Shayateen.**
c) **Seeking refuge with Allah with the prescribed supplications for seeking refuge.**

It was narrated from Abu Sa'eed al-Khudri (رضى الله عنه) that the Messenger of Allah ﷺ prayed Fajr prayer and he (Abu Sa'eed was behind him. He ﷺ recited and got confused in his recitation. When the prayer was over, he said, "If only you could have seen me and Iblees. I grabbed him and kept on trying to strangle him until I felt the coldness of his saliva on these two fingers, the thumb and the one next to it.

Were it not for the prayer of my brother Sulaymaan (عليه سلام), he would have been tied to one of the pillars of the mosque this morning, and the children of Madeenah would have played with him. Whoever among you can prevent him from coming between him and the qiblah, let him do that." [Musand Ahmad]

So, if Shayateen came to the Prophets in order to hurt them and corrupt their worship, and Allah would defend them with that which Allah equipped the Prophets with, like the Dua, Dhikr, worship and struggle by hand, then how about those who are not Prophets?

The Prophet ﷺ subdued the Shayateen from the jinn and mankind with that which Allah had equipped him with from knowledge, actions and the greatest of them is Salaat and struggle, and there are many ahaadeeth of the Prophet ﷺ concerning it. So, he who follows the Prophet ﷺ, then Allah supports him like He supported the Prophets.

As for him, who innovates in the religion, and leaves the prescribed forms of worship to Allah alone and Ittiba (following) to His Prophet ﷺ in that which he ﷺ prescribed for the ummah, and innovates exaggeration with regards to the prophets and the righteous, and commits shirk through them - such is whom the Shaytaan plays with. Allah (سبحانه و تعالى) says, "Verily! He (Shaytaan) has no power over those who believe and put their trust only in their Lord. His power is only over those who obey and follow him (Shaytaan), and those who join partners with Him (Allah)." [Soorah an-Nahl (16): 99-100]

The one who experiences such things should invoke Allah to clarify the situation, ask that man, "Are you such and such?" and then ask him to swear by the greatest swearing. He should read upon him excerpts from the Qur'aan that hurt the Shayateen.

This is like what many worshipers see that the Ka'bah circumambulates around him, and he sees a great throne upon which is a great figure and many individuals going up and down. He thinks that these are the Angels and that the figure is Allah - while it is Shaytaan.

Many people have experienced this and amongst them is the one, whom Allah protected and he realized that it was Shaytaan, this man was Shaikh Abdul-Qadir in his famous story in which he says,

"I was once busy with worship, and I saw a great throne and upon it was light. It said to me, 'O Abdul Qadir! I am your lord. I have made Halaal (permissible) for you that which I made Haraam (impermissible) for others.'

So I asked, 'Are you Allah, the One except Whom there is no true deity? Go away you enemy of Allah.'

So the light dispersed and there prevailed darkness and it said, 'O Abdul-Qadir, You have escaped from me due to your understanding of the religion and knowledge. I have captivated 70 people with this story.'

It was asked, "How did you know that it was Shaytaan?"

Shaikh Abdul-Qadir replied, "By his statement, 'I have made Halaal for you that which I made Haraam for others.' I knew that the Sharee'ah of the Prophet Muhammad ﷺ is neither abrogated nor changed, and also because he said, 'I am your Lord.' He could not say, 'I am Allah - there is no deity worthy of being worshiped except Me.'"

Amongst those (who experience such unusual incidents) are those who believe that the figure is Allah, and he and his companions begin believing that they can see Allah in wakefulness, and their belief is based upon what they see. **Although, they are truthful in what they relate, they do not know that it was Shaytaan.**

This often occurs with groups of ignorant worshipers. One of them thinks that he sees Allah with his own eyes in the world because many of them are shown what he thinks is Allah, while he is Shaytaan. Many people see what they think is a Prophet or a righteous man or Khidr while he is Shaytaan.

It is established in the Saheeh from the Prophet ﷺ, "Whoever sees me in a dream has really seen me, because Shaytaan cannot appear in my image."

[Saheeh al-Bukharee]

This seeing (of Allah's Messenger ﷺ) is in a dream, because seeing (Allah's Messenger ﷺ) during a dream might be true and might be from Shaytaan.

Allah has forbidden Shaytaan from taking the shape of the Prophet in a dream. As for during wakefulness, nobody sees him ﷺ with his eyes in this world. Whosoever thinks that the figure is the dead person, then he has been deceived due to his ignorance. And therefore such incidents never occurred with the Sahabah or those who followed them in good.

Some who have witnessed this or believed in someone who claims to have seen the Prophet ﷺ has believed that one person can be at two places at the same time - he has thus contradicted the sound intellect.

Amongst them are those who say that this is Raqeeqah or Ruhaaniyah, or other explanations for the figure - they do not know that it is a jinn who takes the Prophet's form.

From them are those who think that it is an Angel. An Angel is distinguished from the Jinn in many ways. Amongst the Jinn are disbelievers, sinners and ignorant. From them are believers who submissively follow Prophet Muhammad ﷺ. Many of those who do not know that these are Jinn and Shayateen believe that these are Angels.

Similarly, those who call upon the stars, idols, etc. upon them descend the spirit, which they call the spirit of stars. Some of them believe that these are angels - whereas it is the Jinn and the Shayateen, who are misleading the mushrikeen.

The Shayateen patronize the one, who does what they love; like Shirk, Fisq and sin.

- At times, they inform him about the unseen issues, which he can reveal (to the people).
- Sometimes they hurt the one, who he wants to hurt by killing or afflicting with diseases, etc.
- Sometimes they bring for him someone he wants from mankind.
- Sometimes they steal people's possessions for him like, food, clothes, etc. while he thinks that this is the karamaat of the Awliya.
- Sometimes the Shayateen carry him through the air to far off places, some of them are taken to Makkah one evening and brought back therein. He (the ignorant) thinks this is a karamah, although he has not performed the Hajj of the Muslims; he did not wear the Ihraam, say the talbiyah, perform the tawaaf of the House or go between Safa and Marwa. It is known that this is the greatest misguidance.

From them is he who goes to the Ka'bah to perform tawaaf around the house, he does not take on the Ihram when he passes the meeqat although it is known that he who intends to perform the manasik of Makkah (i.e., Hajj and Umrah), it is not permissible for him to pass the meeqat except in the state of ihram...

This is a broad subject and it includes magic and sorcery which has been explained elsewhere. Mushrikeen who worship the idols, those who resemble them from the Christians, and innovators of this ummah have numerous lengthy stories.

There is no one who gets used to calling upon a dead and seeking help from a prophet or someone else - except that there is a cause for his deviation, like those who call upon them in their absence and seek their help - see someone in his shape or think that it is he (i.e., the dead) in this shape and he says, 'I am such and such.' He talks to them and fulfills some of their needs. They think that the dead whom they sought help from is the one who spoke to them and helped them whereas he is from the Jinn and Shaytaan.

From them is he who says that it is an angel - but the angels don't help the mushrikeen - rather it is the Shayateen who misguide them from the path of Allah. Such incidents and stories occur at places of shirk, and these stories are known to those who are present there and those with whom it occurs.

There are two kinds of ignorant people
- A kind that denies all of it
- A kind that believes that these are the karamaat of the Awliya

The first kind says that this is hallucination and has no reality. So when they say this to group after group, (then) he who has witnessed (such incidents) with his own eyes or he has received news from numerous people who witnessed it, or he is informed by someone whom he does not doubt his truthfulness - then this becomes the greatest reason for the steadfastness of these Mushrikeen innovators, who have seen such incidents and who have received truthful news.

(Likewise), when these people who deny such incidents, (themselves) witness something of this sort, they submit themselves to the one who experiences such things (i.e., the one who performs such unusual acts), and follow him and believe that he is from the Awliya of Allah - although they are aware that he does not offer his obligatory duties to Allah - not even the five daily Salaat - and does not keep away from the prohibitions of Allah, neither illicit acts nor injustice. Rather he might be from the people who are farthest away from the Eeman (faith) and the Taqwa (righteousness) with which Allah has described his Awliya in His (سبحانه و تعالى) saying, "No doubt! Verily, the Awliya of Allah, no fear shall come upon them nor shall they grieve. Those who believed and used to fear Allah much."

[Soorah Yunus (10): 62-63]

So, they see someone - who is farthest from Eeman and Taqwa - revealing unseen matters and performing unusual activities, which they believe are from the karamaat of the pious Awliya of Allah.

- From them is he who renounces Islam and believes that someone who does not pray, rather who does not even believe in the messengers but abuses and belittles them, is from the greatest pious Awliya of Allah.

- From them is he who remains confused, hesitant, doubtful and uncertain - approaching Kufr (disbelief) at one step and approaching Islam at the other - and perhaps he might be nearer to Kufr than Eeman.

The reason for this is that they implied wilaya by that which does not imply wilaya (i.e., they think that the occurrence of unusual events means that the person is a Wali although unusual events are not a sign of wilaya). [Read more about the Karamaat and Awliya on our website, www.qsep.com]

(the reality of these unusual incidents is that) The disbelievers and mushrikeen, magicians and soothsayers have Shayateen who do much more than this for them. "Shall I inform you (O people!) upon whom the Shayateen descend? They descend on every lying (one who tells lies), sinful person." [Soorah ash-Shu'ara (26): 221]

Without doubt such people possess the traits of lying and opposition to the Sharee'ah, they have sin and falsehood in accordance to their distance from the Command and Prohibitions of Allah with which He sent his Messenger ﷺ.

These devilish incidents /acts are a result of their deviation, Shirk, Bidah and ignorance and Kufr and it is a sign and proof of it. The deviant and the ignorant think that it is a result and sign of their Eeman and their wilaya for Allah. Such is because he doesn't have a Furqan (criterion) which distinguishes between the Awliya of Allah and the Awliya of Shaytaan as we have spoken about in, 'al-Furqan bayna Awliya ar-Rahman wa Awliya ash-Shyatan.' (a very informative book of Shaikhul-Islam Ibn Taymiyyah. *translator's note)

(Such is also because) he does not know these situations which he claims to be a proof for wilaya of Allah are achieved by the disbelievers

68

from the mushrikeen and the people of the book - more than those who associate themselves with Islam.

A proof should be something which is particular to that which it proves, and it should not exist without that which it proves. So, if it (i.e., the unusual act) is achieved by the disbelievers, the mushrikeen and the people of the book then it does not necessitate Eemaan, let alone wilaya and it is not specific to wilaya. So, it (i.e., unusual acts) cannot be a proof of wilaya.

The Awliya of Allah are the righteous believers and their karamaat are the fruit of their Eeman and Taqwa and not a fruit of Shirk, Bidah and Fisq. Moreover, the major Awliya use these karamaat as a Hujjah (proof) of the Deen or for the benefit of the Muslims. The thrifty might use it for permissible issues. As for him who helps sin through it then he is being unjust to his own-self while exceeding the bounds of Allah - even if the cause of it is Eeman and Taqwa.

If he who struggles against the enemy, acquires war-booty and then spends it in obedience to Shaytaan then this wealth even if it was acquired through righteous actions - is a curse on him. So, how about if the cause of the unusual activities is Kufr, Fisq and disobedience and moreover it (is used to) call others to Kufr, Fisq and disobedience!! This is the reason why most of their heads have died upon other than Islam, and this is not the place for a lengthy discussion on the subject.

The purpose (of the above discussion) here is that the greatest cause behind the deviation of the mushrikeen is what they witness or hear near the idols like information of the unseen or fulfillment of a need, etc. So, if one witnesses that the grave breaks open and a radiant Shaykh comes out of it and hugs him or speaks to him - then he thinks that it is the buried prophet (or the buried Shaykh), whereas the grave has not cracked open, it is the Shaytaan who acted out that for him, just like he acts out for someone that the wall breaks open and a man comes out of it. It is the Shaytaan who has taken the shape of a man and shows him that he has come out of the wall.

These Shayateen tell the one who sees the Shaytaan emerging from the grave, 'we do not stay in our graves, rather from the time one of us is placed in the grave, he comes out of the grave and walks around amongst the people.' Some of them see that the dead is walking in the funeral and takes him by his hand to places. There are many such incidents which are known to those who know it.

And Allah (سبحانه و تعالى) knows best.

May the peace and blessings of Allah be upon Muhammad, his family, his companions and all those who follow him until the Day of Judgment – Ameen.